Thomas

y

The Greatest Railway Builder in the World

Born November 7, 1805. Died December 8, 1870

Tom Stacey
Great-great-grandson

STACEY INTERNATIONAL

Thomas Brassey 1805-70
The Greatest Railway Builder in the World

published by
Stacey International
128 Kensington Church Street
London W8 4BH
Tel: 020 7221 7166 Fax: 020 7792 9288
E-mail: enquiries@stacey-international.co.uk
Website: www.stacey-international.co.uk

ISBN: 1-905299-09-5

CIP Data: A catalogue record for this book is
available from the British Library

© Tom Stacey 2005

Printing & Binding: Planagraphics Ltd

My special thanks to

Rowena Feilden (née Brassey)
Professor George Huxley
Kenneth Rose, CBE
Ralfe Whistler
Michael Chrimes
Vincent Cronin
Sam Stacey

Thomas Brassey
The Greatest Railway Builder in the World

Kith and kin: -

Consider this son of a Cheshire yeoman farmer, growing up in the tiny village of Buerton – 39 souls and no school, when Thomas was born in 1805 – who was to become the biggest contractor in the world, for well over two decades employing on average some 80,000 men at any time at work in a score of countries on any of four continents, altering decisively the social history of the human race, and notwithstanding many a setback leaving one of the largest English fortunes of the century. Cavour, architect of Italian unity (for which he acknowledged the contribution of Brassey's railways), called him 'one of the most remarkable men I know ... clear-headed, cautious, yet very enterprising, and fulfilling his engagements faithfully'.

Faithfully indeed. So widely trusted was he that, in contrast to so many of his formidable entrepreneurial peers, he could retain the financial resource and reputation to ride out the slump of 1866, four years before his death. Everyone held him in honour and affection: I have encountered no recorded exception – this quiet-spoken master of organisation; a person of astonishing drive, coolness of nerve and unfailing scruple: gentleman in the truest sense, his word his bond, and whose working force all but worshipped him. Do I exaggerate? In the end, I suggest that this is fair deduction, even if deduction it remains. We – or, at least, I – have today virtually none of his purely private, or family, correspondence to draw from; no diaries of his, written reminiscences or love letters. Yet the evidence is of a man growing throughout his life towards a moral stature which the scale of his role invited and invoked. We must allow him that.

No Victorian hero of comparable significance is so unsung today as Thomas Brassey, perhaps in part by dint of the very seamlessness of his character. He was as much the antithesis of Trollop's Augustus Melmotte as he was of Dickens' Gradgrind. Nor is there grist for gossips. Of his duo of (lightweight) book-length biographers to date, writing a century apart, Sir Arthur Helps, commissioned by the family to tell the story immediately after his death in 1870, got permission to dedicate his *Life and Labours of Mr Brassey* to Queen Victoria. 'Your Majesty,' cooed Helps' dedication, 'will find that the late Mr Brassey was an employer after your Majesty's own heart: always solicitous for the well-being of those who served under him; never keeping aloof from them, but using the powerful position of a master in such a manner as to win their affections, and to diminish the distance which is often too great between employer and employee.' It was the same gift as that of Horatio Nelson, killed at Trafalgar the year he was born, with his sailors.

For the sake of plausibility Helps had entreated each of Brassey's three sons to come up with something critical to say of their father. They couldn't. Maybe they were in awe of their recollection of him or of his reputation, unable (because unwilling) to stand back and view him in the round; maybe they hadn't known him all that closely since he had so little time to spend with them. Certainly his activities were too complex, his operations too ubiquitous and skills too various, to be shared round the family table. Yet by all the evidence, he *was* a family man. I think I find that through his sons he came to dream. For their part, when he was gone, they had virtually no scrap of the negative to offer. No more do I. There are facts to pass you, as I have gathered then; a few deductions therefrom; and a vivid slither of 19th century English history which our age is reluctant to admire. Yet stand by to admire.

Brassey was known for an evenness of temperament and his thoughtfulness. Here was a unwaveringly conscientious man, loyal to family for sure, but with his loyalty pledged no less fervently – without proclaiming it – to the call of his professional life and those whom he carried with him in it: horizontally, as one might visualise it, to the most remotely scattered of his workmen and vertically to the clients and potentates his projects served. He was famously steady in adversity (of which he had his share); caring and forgiving; equable, and unshakeably straight. He hated to dismiss an employee, unless for flagrant indiscipline or indolence or disloyalty. If a man failed in one role, he would give him a chance in another. Slow to chide others, he was reluctant to pass the blame, however justified. By his ethic, his means of grace, the buck stopped with Thomas Brassey.

I have heard myself declaring that among endowments for success in business the *sine qua non* are the twin demons Greed and Fear, in inner roles of equivalent authority. In my great-great-grandfather, a colossus of Victorian commerical enterprise and entrepreneurial daring, the role of

Greed is played by Probity and Commitment, and Fear by Grit and Pluck. Of course he sought and needed financial success. Yet we cannot but sense his first motive for ensuring, as best he could, that his projects brought a profit was to enable him to bid for the next and keep his army of men in gainful work.

In private life he was widely charitable; in the conduct of his business open-handed. He disdained contention. Part of his temperament he evidently shared with Robert Walpole who famously claimed he shed the cares of his office as he shed his clothes for bed: a critical innerly dismantling. 'Don't take your troubles to your pillow,' Brassey would counsel others. In the priorities of his values his was a house built on rock. He had no side that I can detect, no vainglory at all, unless one were to read into his recorded comment that 'no one shall say that Thomas Brassey's word is not his bond' a fragment of self-commendation. He brushed aside invitations to stand for Parliament, and had no interest in public honours. Accepting with due grace the insignia of the *Légion d'Honneur* from Louis Napoleon of France and the Order of St Maurice and St Lazarus from King Victor Emmanuel of Italy, he soon mislaid the medals, requiring to send out for duplicates to please his wife: 'Mrs Brassey will be glad to possess all these crosses.'

As for Maria Brassey's own comment on him when she was widowed, the term she chose fits no tycoon: 'other-worldly'. Her eldest son Tom's description was likewise unpredictable: 'easy going'. I guess he meant, in the language of our time, 'unflappable'. Brassey seems to have affected others with this inner calm and stature. The comment on him by one of his navvies has come down the years: 'If he'd been a boxer he'd have got the belt. If he'd been a parson he'd have become a bishop.' When he was laying down the load at 65, wracked by cancer, a group of his north country workforce who had heard of this final illness walked for days, gathering their mates with them, to assemble at his home and there to stay in vigil till the end.

That was the early winter of 1870. By that date Brassey had been responsible for the building of about a third of the railways in Britain, three-quarters of France's, major rail lines in Denmark, Norway, Belgium and Switzerland; in Moldavia, Saxony, Bohemia, Hungary, Transylvania, and the imperial motherland of Austria itself; in Spain and Italy; Poland and Russia; Syria and Persia; in India, Australia, Canada and Argentina; and, crucially for Britain at war, in Allied-occupied Crimea. That, in all, was 6,415 miles of railways, together with associated docks, brickworks, stations, and drainage works. His were the world's longest tunnels, the deepest cuttings, the biggest bridges, including the unprecedented 2-mile Victoria bridge across the St Lawrence River at Montreal, and the great gorge spans of the rivers of upper India: all and everything to the highest standards of that time and indeed, for most of it, of this time too – standards which were never less than matters of life and death. He played a role in the development of steamships (including I K Brunel's *Great Eastern*), in mines, in locomotive factories, marine telegraphy, and water supply and sewage systems (as for the burgeoning cities of Calcutta or Rio de Janeiro).

He visited virtually every project he had in hand in Britain, Europe, and Canada, in many cases repeatedly. The vitality and drive of this 'easy going', 'other-worldly' man may be judged from the testimony of his brother-in-law and frequent business associate, Henry Harrison: 'I have known him come direct from France to Rugby' – crossing the Channel overnight from le Havre – 'and engage in the office in London the whole day. He would then come down to Rugby by the mail train, arriving at midnight, and it was his practice to be in the [railway] works by 6 o'clock the next morning. He would frequently then walk from Rugby to Nuneaton, a distance of 16 miles. Arriving at Nuneaton in the afternoon, he would proceed the same night to Tamworth; and the next morning he would be out on the road so soon that he had the reputation among his staff of being first man at the works. Thence to Stafford, walking the greater part of the distance, and that same day to inspect the works on the Lancaster-Carlisle line he was building.' He would be walking, not riding, to be on the same level with the men at work – men, in this instance, living in turf huts, 30 to each, for whom at Shap he built a church and a school.

Can we frame this phenomenon?

∞ ∞ ∞

This farmer's boy's earliest education, so far as we can surmise, was at home with his parents and, perhaps, a governess. That would have been in the hamlet of Buerton, near Aldford (where he was christened) just south of Cheshire, or the village of Bulkeley, half a day's ride to the east, where the senior branch of the Brasseys had been resident in the pleasant black-and-white Bulkeley Grange since Tudor times or earlier. At the age of twelve he went as a boarder to Mr Harling's school at Chester. He was not noted as a scholar, yet an aptitude for mental arithmetic was remarked on. At 16 he was apprenticed to a local land agent named Lawton, who just then was surveying for the building of Telford's A5 highroad to Holyhead. In the cut and thrust of real life he proved himself a fast learner, for at 21 Lawton made him a partner. Their next enterprise was in Birkenhead. There he was shortly to borrow money from his father to set up a brickworks to build the new customs house for that fast-growing little port. It was at Birkenhead that he struck up with the family of Joseph Harrison, a forwarding agent, who had two sons (Henry and George) and two daughters. In the younger, Maria, he was to find a soulmate. A courtship was entered upon.

Not far to the east, in 1827, George Stephenson, creator of the steam locomotive, was about to build the world's first commercial passenger railway: the Manchester to Liverpool line. Stephenson's 30-mph *Rocket* was soon to grip the country's imagination. Up to then the 'rail-way', when not derided by the wiseacres of Parliament and the gentry as new-fangled, dangerous and destined to fail, was seen at best as a means of shifting heavy industrial goods and materials short distances from one site to another. It so happened that young Brassey had the management of a quarry at Stourton when Stephenson came looking for stone for his pioneering rail line's Sankey viaduct. Stephenson was swift to recognise a young man of the right cast. With Stephenson's guidance, Brassey bid for a contract to build the Dutton rail viaduct near Warrington. The bid failed, but his zest had been fired and the youthful entrepreneur had budded. He married his steady Maria when he was 26, and they set themselves up in a house he built himself in Birkenhead's Park Road South. Thus rooted and emboldened, in 1833 he grasped the next opportunity to tender for a railway contract. This was to build the Penkridge viaduct between Stafford and Wolverhampton, plus ten miles of that line. This time he won. He was 29. Things were soon to change – for the Thomas Brasseys and many a fellow man.

He was backed by Dixon and Wardle's bank in Northgate Street, Chester, where he had opened his first account eight years earlier. Little did the manager imagine – so Brassey's rollicking memorialist John Millar has speculated[1] – that within a dozen years this soft-spoken young client would

---

[1] *See* my sources.

have the bank handling more money for his companies than was passing through many a European country's national treasury of that era. His partner in the Penkridge deal was Joseph Locke, a Fellow of the Royal Society and an engineer of outstanding gifts five years Brassey's senior. Locke had fallen out with George Stephenson over the pioneer's wayward imprecision in the critical matter of surveying, not least when two teams set to boring a tunnel from both ends were to meet in the middle … or not to meet. Brassey was always to prefer to work in partnership, and in Locke he had found a master of the craft, a veritable genius at laying out a line, and a friend for life. Penkridge Viaduct stands today, fully serviceable. Brassey was once asked how long he built his works to last: 'Ninety-nine years?' the enquirer volunteered. 'At ninety-nine years,' came the reply, 'it should be as good as when it was built.' All of Brassey's British lines, bridges, viaducts and tunnels not Beeching-ised into disuse are today just about the same, and as good, as when he built them.

And next, 1834, with the indefatigable Locke, he won the contract for a piece of the main London to Southampton line; that is to say, the capital's first link to a major ocean-facing port. This was to prove a significant advance no less for Brassey than for railways. The job was well done. Thereafter, railway contracts in Britain followed thick and fast: Chester to Crewe, Glasgow to Greenock, Manchester to Sheffield … A railway mania was taking hold in Britain; yet to be sure many a line was dangerously speculative, and the projects were haphazard and piecemeal. The French, by contrast, slower off the mark and far less experienced, were approaching the railway *réalité* with caution but also with central planning. Each new line in Britain indeed needed Parliamentary approval, a laborious and expensive procedure; but that did not mean much coherent matrix: each line was the consequence of its own entrepreneurial wheeze with its customary freight of wishful thinking. In France, central government itself took the initiative. Brassey respected France's endeavour at overall network planning. In 1841 came the first prospect of a key French railway link.

This was an 82-mile line between Paris and the Seine's ocean-reaching port at Rouen. Only the British had undertaken such a major railway project till then. Brassey and his British rival, the experienced William Mackenzie, eleven years his senior, submitted their separate tenders which both (seemingly under the guidance of Locke) quoted an identical cost per mile: £15,700 (about £800,000). The French bidders came in with offers way higher and were soon out of the running. But both the British competitors knew their business and each was reluctant to underbid the other. In the event, Brassey linked with Mackenzie as his partner. With the Rothschilds at hand to capitalise the project, the Brassey-led consortium secured the contract[1].

For France and Thomas Brassey there followed a period of astonishing expansion: Orleans all-but-300 miles to Bordeaux, Rouen to le Havre, Amiens to Boulogne. Meanwhile, to celebrate the completion, ahead of schedule, of that first major French line, Paris-Rouen, Brassey characteristically sat down 600 of his work force to an open-air banquet. The assembly was ringed by French cavalry in theatrical dread of the English navvies – in the metaphor of the new trade – letting off steam. (The men behaved decorously enough.) Within sixteen years of his entry onto the French scene, beginning with Mackenzie as partner, Brassey had built three-quarters of the entire railway network of France, with his British corps of experienced labourers spearheading the workforce on each of the projects. By the end of the 1840s Mackenzie's health was failing, and in 1851 he was dead.

∞ ∞ ∞

The yoemen Brasseys had always prided themselves on their Norman provenance, tracing themselves from an ancestor from the Lower Normandy town of Brécey who crossed with William of Normandy in 1066. Atavistic pride in the Norman root was, however, less of an influence in bidding for, and successfully completing, that seminal foreign contract than Thomas' very own Maria. The upwardly mobile young Harrisons of Birkenhead had grown up to speak French. It was a parental stroke of educational foresight. Given her own linguistic accomplishment, Maria brought her man the confidence to make a pitch for the opportunity. Thomas himself risked no spoken French (the Emperor Louis Napoleon conversed in English when he later dined Brassey in

---

[1] Methods of financing the buildings of railways were by now assuming certain formulae. One entailed the client part-paying the contractor in bonds in the projected railway. On these bonds, a contractor whose judgment on the future profitability of the line was trusted could raise loans from a merchant bank with which to pay for the labour and the materials. Within a decade and a half, Brassey would risk financing an entire line (London-Portsmouth) himself, to sell outright to the highest bidder.

Paris); but when a distinguished French engineer, witnessing the British on the job, was quoted as exclaiming '*Ces Anglais! Comme ils travaillent!*' the compliment could hardly have passed him by. The Brasseys' French connexion was destined to endure.

In Thomas' career Maria was ever game. She had soon borne him three sons: Thomas in 1836; my great-grandfather Henry in 1840; and Albert, in Rouen, in 1844. (A fourth son had died in infancy.) Since their first home in Birkenhead – and it was Maria who spurred Thomas into seizing his opportunities far beyond the environs of Birkenhead – the family had already moved four times in England: to Stafford, Kingston-upon-Thames, Winchester and Fareham. She supervised the crating up and shunting off to whatever new site best allowed for his own oversight of the new big contracts. The moves must have entailed a ruthless weeding-out of anything the family didn't need. Maybe this is how the letters went. There exists a rather posed and uncharacteristically dandified portrait by Frederick Newenham done about this time of the young contractor seated cross-legged in a leather chair with a quill pen in hand and over-flowing waste-paper basket. (He shared my habit of filing on the floor.) Yet if all this moving homes must have interfered with the family's chances of building a circle of friends, he was not one to let ambition sacrifice closeness with a treasured family. With the original French assignment, the family had up-sticked to Vernon, in Normandy, and thence to Rouen and to Paris and back to Rouen, before at last returning to a more or less permanent London base in Lowndes Square in Belgravia. Maria was with her man all the way: unfalteringly supportive of Thomas's career, a source of stability and sense we can only guess at.

Brassey brought to his work such gifts! To start with, he had first-hand knowledge of so many aspects of the task ahead, all the hazards and complexities of building a railway – the vital factor of surveying and the assessment of land surface and the rock crust beneath; the plotting of the route; the treachery of the water-table, the volatility of soil and sand and peat and clay, the intractability of bogland; the gradients, bridges, viaducts, cuttings, tunnels, embankments; the quality and quantity of materials as also of skills, the time-saving precision of teamwork; the selection and allocation of men for this, that, and all else; and no doubt familiarity with what in modern parlance in the construction industry is known as Murphy's law: *if it can go wrong it will go wrong*. On the basis of a preliminary survey, ever widening experience, and much shrewdness, he could create at speed a detailed prospectus, doing most of the sums in his head and calculating an approximate cost per mile or kilometre. With the contract secured, there came into play his gift of picking the right men as his engineers and managers in the virtual certainty from early in his career that the cream of the key professions wanted to work for him. One further gift was, I suggest, unique to himself, an innate benison singled out by his first biographer: the way he handled his vast labour force – his navvies and their gangers. Those men and the inspiration he brought them were his golden asset. His relationship with them had a unique style, and a shared depth. My grandmother, Thomas' granddaughter Beatrice, told me the one certain thing she knew about him: *They all said he was wonderful with the men.*

Who were the men? In the early days they were mostly English, from the Midlands and the north, bevies inherited from the canal-builders like Telford. It was from the canal-building profession's charting of waterway routes they earned their name, *navigators*: navvies. England was awash with men seeking work – men from families which had drifted into the cities and towns with the enclosure of common farmland in the late 18th century. Many had found work in the new mines and mills. The ending of the canal boom had thrown large numbers into the pool of unemployment. For them, the building of railways was a gift of life.

Samuel Smiles, that tireless definer and chronicler of the Victorian ethic, describes the navvy:

> 'He usually wore a white felt hat with a brim turned up, a velvet or jean square-tailed coat, a scarlet plush waistcoat with little black spots, and a high-coloured kerchief round his herculean neck when, as often happened, it was not left entirely bare. His corduroy breeches were retained in position by a leather strap round the waist, and were tied and buttoned at the knee, displaying a solid calf, and a foot encased in strong high-laced boots.'

It was not long before the English contingent of navvies was joined by Scots, Irish and Welsh, each speaking in the camps their Celtic tongue but with enough English to get along. The Irish proportion increased with onset of the potato famine from 1845. For any Brassey-led consortia, they would work anywhere and endure severe hardship. They knew he would never let them down, never keep them waiting for their pay – on average per week, in mid-century, £1 direct to the families of each navvy and £1.16s to the navvy himself on site. They would never find him unresponsive to their needs or indifferent to their plight. The work force were provided with 2lbs of beef per head a day – plus the rest of their food and their tobacco; their clothing (27 items, including bedclothes); and unless they were lodging out, their shelter, their fuel, their lamps and, on many a project, a lending library. They bought their own beer. When native labour came to be recruited on foreign contracts, the British Isles contingent found itself earning double the others' since as a rule their productivity was about twice that of the native worker. The British navvies knew the ropes; they were formidably muscled and highly motivated; they knew they were earning, yard by yard, a share of any bonus on offer for early completion. They were fiercely proud of their superiority. It went with Empire.

Spoil from the cuttings and the tunnels provided most of the ballast for the embankments. Temporary lines of a narrow gauge were laid down to shift the spoil in horse-drawn wagons, by means of which the wagons were brought to where the track began a downward incline towards where the ballast was to be tipped. At that late point, the horse was unhitched to veer away, freeing the loaded wagon to bowl down the slope and ram a sleeper laid across the rails, thus shooting forward the wagon's contents of earth or rock into the required region of earthwork, where the shovelmen got to work. It was a formula for speed of operation if also for accidents among the unwary, and casualties were not low. Cuttings required gunpowder as did, of course, tunnels, which were invariably hazardous. Perilous in a very different way were the coffer dams and compressed-air caissons essential to bridge-building. Brassey undoubtedly cared about the casualties, and had his codes of practice which he would hope to engender among his subcontractors. The men knew what they were in for. By the practice of today, every director of a Victorian company building railways, however scrupulous, would have been in court on charges of corporate manslaughter, and spent their profits on the law.

Yet the men of the day had the sense that they were Titans, and confirmed the illusion in their cups at the end of the day, which is where most of their wages went. Men of collective muscle and with women scarce tend towards restiveness and much booze. On the Brassey track pushing north to Carlisle in 1846 the English assaulted the Irish, who fought back: the military had to be called in, and the ringleader was deported to enrich the blood of young Australia.

Thomas Carlyle described the navvies working on the line running north to Edinburgh as 'sunk three-fold deeper in brutality by the three-fold wages they are getting'. Brassey treasured them like his extended family, sought to value each in his way as a specialist, using that very word in his dictum: 'Let each man keep to his speciality.' No man was not special. He knew personally many of his men all the way down the scale of authority: many of the 'gangers' or foremen and the navvies themselves, to whom he would walk over to greet by name and with a handshake, discussing with them in earnest detail the techniques and frustrations of each one's task, weighing up how the job might be done that much better, or conditions eased, or rations improved; then instructing accordingly.

All of this commissioning and mastering of Brassey's labour force was conducted on a vast scale. By the mid-1840s the numbers had risen to 50,000, by the later 1840s to 80,000. Of that number, all those engaged in British homeland contracts were, naturally, of British Isles stock, and so also for most of his early contracts on the continent of Europe. In France he would operate his projects with up to 11 language groups, which included Irish (Erse), Gaelic, Welsh and English, often separately billeted. The British Isles contingents played a role in varying proportions further afield – in Persia, India, and later on in Canada. In Australia they were British enough; even in Argentina, immigrant British were on the scene. Brassey had conjured a race of hard-handed professionals who would endure the discomforts and face the hazards, and as often as not were already comrades, loyal to one another and intensely loyal to the project and to the top master, Brassey himself. He was repeatedly arriving on site, and the men – in their droves – felt not only that they knew him, but that he knew them and valued them.

Each of the Brassey consortia engaged in the multifarious activities of creating the new tracks – from quarrying to bridge-building – worked through tiers of managers, foremen and timekeepers under what evolved as the butty gang system, the 'gang' often being paid an agreed price for a given piece of work and the money shared equally among the navvies with an extra sum for the ganger. At the top of the scale, Brassey's agent on site would be have overall responsibility for a project. The agent was invariably a man of wide capability. He would work for a fee and a percentage of the profits, which would be calculated on the all-in contract price, itself usually hedged on the one side with heavy penalties for being late on finishing, and vista-ed on the other by inducements for finishing early.

Similarly having 'a piece of the action', in today's commercial jargon, would often be those filling the other pivotal function in any given project, the chief engineers. Brassey's chosen engineers included George Stephenson's son Robert, Joseph Locke, Hawkshaw in India, I K Brunel, Fitzgibbon in Australia, Ross and Hodges in Canada, Woods in Argentina, McClean, Joseph Harrison Jr, Henry Harrison, and William Heap. Brassey worked again and again with the same engineers and agents, growing familiar with the strengths and fallibilities of each.

∞ ∞ ∞

This Brassey endeavour was spanning the globe. Yet for every contract he was awarded, he and his senior team had assessed, and bid for, half a dozen others. He once calculated that he had tendered for £150 million's worth of business he was not awarded – say, £7.5 billion in today's money. In building railways, the hazards of the unforeseen, indeed the unforeseeable, were legion. When a lot of business was for the taking, there was little merit in cutting a corner on the tender's calculations to shave a price; yet many a contractor, for the sake of a competitive edge, would do just that ... and rue it soon thereafter when the earth's crust through which the line would run turned out to be, say, not chalk but whinstone. Even Brassey could frame his bid on the most thorough survey obtainable and, once accepted, shake the client's hand on it only to find the unforeseen conspiring to bring him a loss, at times on a brutal scale. Virtually every project involved a gamble. Yet Brassey would never fail a client, never never skimp on a job, never welsh on a deal.

Brassey's methods and performance were earning for his fellow countrymen a formidable reputation around the world for workmanship and their work ethic, such as would endure a century. As the assignments multiplied, local 'foreign' workforces were recruited and trained to imitate English norms and scruple and thoroughness, and to mirror English attitudes of faith in management and allegiance to the enterprise. That the men and clients alike should learn to put their trust in Brassey-led consortia became his cardinal requirement in the conduct of business, and his trump card. Did not the clients deserve a return on their investment? Of course; yet no less nor more than the labourers deserved their hire. For Thomas Brassey there grew to be a driven sanctity to all this. He infected those around him with it. If they would earn for him, he would earn for them.

A dramatic episode illustrates this ethic at work. In 1866, at the height of the Prussian assault on the Austro-Hungarian empire, Brassey was engaged in fulfilling a contract for the Austrian government for the building of a major line from Cracow to Lemberg as they were then known (today's Krakov in Poland, and Lviv – *aka* Lvov – in Ukraine). The contract had been agreed under a sky of cloudless peace; but now, in the midst of its fulfilment, was all-out war … and the railwaymen, on the other side of the fighting line where the Imperial forces were engaged in desperate battle with the Prussian invaders, were due their wages. Brassey's agent for the project, a certain Victor Ofenheim, had drawn the wages, in coin, from the bank in Vienna. That line, already mostly built, was understandably inoperative, and its brand new engines duly mothballed until peace should dawn.

Ofenheim was imbued with the Brassey code. In a shed in Cracow he found a discarded Birkenhead-built locomotive. With a rattle of coinage he persuaded an elderly and reluctant local engine driver to get up steam, loaded the bags of currency into the cab of the loco, and flat out, at 50 mph, roared upon the scene of battle. God alone knew what obstruction lay across the track, or what track had been ripped up. From their cab, agent and driver saw wounded stragglers flinging themselves out of the loco's thundering path and alarmed horses rearing and bolting. Immediately ahead, amid cannons booming, opposing cavalry and infantry were engaged in hand-to-hand combat. Ofenheim gave a blast on the whistle, and with smoke belching and furious pistons the lone engine swept through the astonished soldiery. In their encampment near Lviv, or Lemberg, the gangers and their navvies got their pay. When surviving Imperial officers relayed an account of this, word of it reached the Emperor Franz Joseph, emerging into a somewhat humiliating peace. He sent for Ofenheim and enquired, 'Who is this Mr Brassey, the English contractor, for whom men are to be found who will work with such zeal and risk their lives?' Locating Brassey, he presented him with the Cross of the Iron Crown.

The construction business calls for men of strong nerve and high caution. Thomas Brassey possessed both qualities temperamentally and physically. He thought nothing of crossing a 50-foot drop along a 12-inch plank. In a tunnel he was inspecting on Mantes-Cherbourg line, scaffolding collapsed beneath him, shaking him violently and breaking Joseph Locke's shin-bone in two places. He was seldom far from the action. When casualties occurred, he would see to it that every next-of-kin received a letter of individual condolence, many such a letter written by himself. At times the casualties were on a formidable scale. Probably the worst single catastrophe took place in 1857 when the Hauenstein tunnel collapsed during the building of the Basle to Olten line; 52 men were buried alive. In India, and in Canada too, there was cholera to contend with. Dysentery and malaria, in the subtropics and tropics, were a recurring threat, and in Argentina tuberculosis. The Delhi-Amritsar line involved the perilous bridging of the vast gorge of the Sutlej and the equally vast Jumna, a river with a disquieting propensity for changing course. Loss of life in some measure was as inevitable as in battle.

While he kept a London office, Brassey never employed a personal secretary. To seek his pending tray, best look into his head. His memory for the details of the work in train was prodigious and precise. He travelled with a personal valet, Isidore, and latterly with a devoted cashier, Tapp. But he wrote all his letters in his own hand. Wherever he went he carried a bag with his writing equipment. His oft-times partner Joseph Locke has recorded how, on a rare day out shooting in Scotland, his friend's temporary absence was noted: Brassey had sneaked away to write letters in a shepherd's hut. Another companion, Dr Burnett, with Brassey in Italy, recalls how – after dining at 9 pm and he and the rest of the party retiring to bed – he, Burnell, awoke in the morning to find 31 letters written overnight by the master contractor to agents and subcontractors all over the world. Such was virtually his daily practice: the exercise of a very private vow and discipline. Clearly Brassey came to require of himself a commitment of which the fulfilment gave his life its meaning: a commitment to the project in the context of the advance of civilisation, and to the men as (I venture) deserving fellow human souls. In the exercise of that integrity, surely, he found his best peace. He was the man responsible, whatever befell.

Drive and single-minded commitment, yes; but never a raised voice, never a threat or high-handedness, never panic. He eschewed contention. Much of the work would be done by subcontractors who would present their skills and offer their prices. When the deal was struck, it was not infrequently the case that the subcontractor had underestimated and would come to see he was heading for a loss. When next visiting the site, Thomas Brassey would hear the fellow out, weigh up the genuineness of his plight and, if genuine it was, make up the loss himself, often with a subcontractor thrown in. Such an action would win the subcontractor's undying allegiance. A different scruple applied should his own consortium have underestimated the cost of project, or met with unforeseeable obstacles which could be overcome only at grievous additional expense. Brassey would hold to his agreed quotation and draw from his personal funds. Such occurred, for example, with the building of the Bilbao railway in northern Spain, in 1858, when torrential rain swept away a bridge and a stretch of the line. (His agent on that occasion, Bartlett, had been obliged to employ a brigandish Carlist subcontractor, who surrounded his villa and threatened, in unquestionable earnest, personally to kill every man in it 'like a fly' unless he was paid at the inflated rate he now demanded.) Without demur, Brassey reached into his pocket to make good and rebuild what was lost. On the demanding Rouen to le Havre line (1843-6) a 100-foot high, 26-arch viaduct was built at Barentin. Brassey had been dissatisfied with the quality of the mortar which was provided locally as his contract required. The elegant viaduct was visited and praised by France's Minister of Works. Shortly thereafter, dawn had not yet broken on January 10, 1846. There had been several days of teeming rain. At 6 am the fifth arch from the Rouen end collapsed; within two minutes one arch after another had crumbled into the valley beneath. On hearing of this catastrophe Brassey's opening words were, 'The first thing is to build it up again.' This he did at once, this time using lime of his own choice. There were no recriminations on his part, despite a scarcely justified anti-Anglo-Saxon hullabaloo in the French press. He paid for the whole thing himself, at a cost of over £1.5 million in today's values.

It seemed he was all but spurred by setbacks, by the test of his calmness and ingenuity and resolve in the restoration of whatever had befallen the project, and in the completion of the job.

The biggest financial loss for Thomas Brassey was to be incurred on the most formidable constructional achievement of his life. This was the building of the 541-mile Grand Trunk Railway of Canada. Commissioned by the Government of Canada in 1852, the main stretch was to run from the city of Quebec, at the head of the Gulf of St Lawrence, to Toronto on the north-western shore of Lake Ontario. The route from Quebec ran south of the St Lawrence River, crossing the mighty river at Montreal, from where it would follow the northern bank to Kingston at the north-eastern end of Lake Ontario, and thence to Toronto. A linked line pushed the route eastwards from Toronto to Detroit. The Grand Trunk Railway was to be the longest railway yet built in the world.

Brassey had teamed up with Sir Morton Peto and Peto's brother-in-law, Edward Betts. The egregious Peto had inherited a modest construction business from a bachelor uncle, with whom he had started as a bricklayer's apprentice. He had been a young man on the move, helping to plan and build Hungerford Market, the Reform Club in Pall Mall, Nelson's Column and a number of West End theatres. By the age of thirty he was rich enough to buy, in 1843, the Somerleyton estate in Suffolk from Lord Sidney Osborne. He dreamed up Somerleyton Hall as a pleasure dome sufficient to impress Kublai Khan: with the beguilement of open walls and over-arching glass domes, you were meant not to know (at least, in summer) whether you were indoors or out. Corridors ended in ferny grottoes where fountains played. The writer W G Sebald has described Peto 'an industrial impresario'. His brother-in-law Betts, growing comparably moneyed in railways, was meanwhile creating his own palatial extravaganza in Preston Hall in Kent.

Sharing the financial risk with these two, the unflamboyant Thomas Brassey, feet-on-the-ground and quietly Anglican, took up the contract to turn the vision of the Grand Trunk Railway into a reality. His trio brought in a fourth partner in the person of Sir William Jackson, with whom Brassey had worked in Piedmont: it was Jackson who assessed the scale of the work, much of it through virgin forest and in the certainty of ferocious winter cold and heavy snowfalls. Brassey now recalled from Canada his brother-in-law George Harrison, who had been over there detailing the engineering requirement, to direct the laying of the groundwork for the English command centre.

In May 1853 he and Harrison were ready to launch the project. For the vast assignment, they determined that a new plant should be established along the dockside at Birkenhead to provide virtually everything of iron, steel, copper and brass the project would need, including that for the prospective spanning of the St Lawrence. It was to be called Canada Works.

On May 29, a Friday, Harrison toured the dock area looking for a suitable piece of ground for an extensive factory site alongside which a quay could be built for loading ocean-going vessels. By lunchtime he had found a site to suit the purpose well enough. That afternoon Harrison spent an hour and a half doing his scale sketches; on these, by the next morning, he had been offered a price by his preferred builder. That afternoon he took the train to London to see Brassey and thrash out the costs and the broad logistics. Sunday was for Church and the family roast. By the Monday afternoon Harrison had returned to Liverpool and on his brother-in-law's behalf had bought the Birkenhead acreage. Bricklaying for the main factory began on Wednesday June 4, five days after Harrison had first set eyes on the land.

The principal blacksmiths' shop was provided with 40 furnaces, anvils, and steam hammers. In the smaller shop were to be manufactured the locomotive wheels. The fitting shop was designed for the manufacture of 40 locomotives a year, a rate whereby 300 engines were to be produced over the next eight years. The machine shop, equipped with Whitworth lathes (for screws), was 900 feet in length, and comprised iron and brass foundries, blacksmiths, coppersmiths, fabrication shop, and woodwork and pattern shops. There were three furnaces dedicated to heating rivets, a furnace for angle-irons and T-irons, eight punching and shearing machines, two rivet-making machines, and two riveting machines. There was also, let us note, a well-stocked library and reading room for all the workforce.

The first locomotive was given its trial in May 1854 – tactfully named *Lady Elgin* after the wife of the Governor-General of Canada. Wood-burning, with a 5ft 6in wheel gauge, her cylinder bore was 15in, and the depth of her pistons 20in. She had 175 'lutes' in the smokebox. The diameter of her leading wheels was 3ft 6in and of the trailing wheels 6ft. She was designed for a cruising speed of 40 mph. Lady Elgin in the flesh could scarcely have been sweeter. By the end of 1854, ten such locomotives had reached Quebec. Engines and carriages alike were provided with the bogies such as had become standard on North American railways – an English invention whose swivelling mechanism allowed for instant yielding, horizontally and laterally, to handle the North American continent's somewhat rougher tracks as compared with those of Europe.

The mastering challenge of the project was to be Montreal's Victoria Bridge – at almost two miles in length by far the longest bridge in the world at that time, and to this day (I believe) the world's longest of tubular steel yet built. Its hundreds of thousands of components were all to be made in Birkenhead or elsewhere in the Midlands and north-east England under specifications provided by Brassey's team, each tagged and packed in order at Canada Works, and in all requiring over 3 million punched holes.

The bridge today carries a plaque to Thomas Brassey as its constructor, and Robert Stephenson as its designer, a testimonial on which my eyes first fell with due pride over half a century ago. The St Lawrence flows powerfully at Montreal, at an average speed of seven knots. Every winter, from November, it freezes over; every spring, in the thaw, as I have witnessed myself, vast blocks of ice ram the piers and the river rises by 20 feet or more. Given the depth and pace of the river, building the piers was going to make huge demands on the constructors. An unexpected challenge was the sheer size of the free-standing boulders which cluttered the river bed and which had to be lifted before the coffer dams could be pile-driven into place or the compressed-air caissons sunk, for the pier foundations to be dug into a dry bed. The journal *The Engineer* reported that one such boulder weighed 24.5 tons.

Building the 24 piers themselves required 2,713,000 cubic feet of hard limestone. A source of such stone was found at a site some 16 miles up-river on land owned by the Mohawk Indians of the Iroquois Federation. James Hodges, as site engineer, needed the Mohawks' permission before quarrying could begin, and a meeting was arranged between him and thirteen elders of the tribe. The elders[1] were reluctant to negotiate: Hodges' sheer youthfulness demeaned them. Only when that gifted engineer satisfied them that he was fully forty years of age would they deign to talk. Eventually, the volume of the stone cut for the piers of the bridge was such as to cover a field of six acres to a depth of eleven feet. For their part, several of the neighbourhood Mohawks themselves joined the labour force, so establishing the northern Amerindians' reputation as the most sure-footed high altitude construction teamsters on the planet.

Frustrations mounted. Cholera erupted in 1854 among the bridge's sub-contracted gangers; there were several strikes. A mass of floating logs – Canada's greatest source of contemporary wealth – destroyed the coffer dam built for Pier 13. The railway had now reached the bridge site from the eastern seaboard, in the face of formidable challenges. As the project encountered each new obstacle the Peto-Brassey-Betts consortium ran ever lower on funds. A new-fangled machine, the steam-traveller, was improvised to assist on the bridge. Thirteen hundred feet in length, over 50 feet high

---

[1] among whom the name Stacey featured prominently, the men being descendants of a certain settler's son, John Stacey, seized as a teenager by the Mohawks across the American border in 1735.

and 60 feet wide, it moved on rails supported by timber scaffolding. This behemoth, operated by one man, could stack with precision blocks of stone to a weight of ten tons. It had handled over 70,000 tons of stone before the world's longest bridge was done. Meanwhile the metalwork was being rivetted into place. Each 'tube' – a squared box-girder – was provided with its own plan on which was shown the position of every T-bar, angle-iron, keelson and coverplate. To each such tube belonged 4,926 pieces, or 9,852 for a pair (they were used in pairs). Every piece of this most complex Meccano set in the history of Man had been punched, stamped and coded to fit the design at Birkenhead, loaded into a variety of commissioned clippers and steam-driven vessels, unloaded at Quebec 2,630 miles across the ocean, moved by rail a further couple of hundred miles to the site, where they were meticulously stacked and labelled in readiness for assemblage. The central span comprised 10,309 components in which had been punched (in Birkenhead) nearly half a million holes. As the bridge was a-building the precision had to be faultless. Hodges left his testimony. 'Not one piece required alteration, neither was a hole punched wrong.'

Meanwhile, the railway itself was being energetically advanced westwards and costs were mounting alarmingly. Labour was scarce, and consequently dear. Conditions for the men were dire, above all in winter when temperatures could drop to minus 40 degrees Fahrenheit. Brassey was reaching deeper into his own pocket, and Peto becoming indebted to most of the financial houses in London. Shortage of capital led to a shortage of rolling stock for that section of the railway already operable. In England a Gauge Commission had entered the scene from 1845, and its respect for Brunel's preference for a wide gauge in the (mistaken) interest of safety, clouded the issue. The quango had misled the Canadian government into favouring a gauge of 5ft 6in which was incompatible with the Americans' (and prevailingly British) 4ft 8ž in. This necessitated the expensive and laborious transfer of cargo moving between one system and another, in the teeth of competition from river and lake steamers.

With problems mounting, Brassey crossed the Atlantic in 1855, two years into the work. He arrived by way of New York where his reputation had run ahead of him. They received him there as a giant of global enterprise. Special trains were put on for him, for the American magnates of the day to outdo each others' hospitality and pick his brains. They knew nothing of his ominous deficit mounting further north. One of the severer tests of a man's character is to maintain outer and inner composure when, while a cynosure of general admiration, he is well aware of the precariousness of his reputation. Brassey surely knew that in the throat of praise and adulation there is seldom absent a muffled undertone of envy and its brother *schadenfreude*.

He kept his cool, and for so long as he was in America he set himself to learn what he could from his hosts' experience. Two perceptions, subtly related, may be attributed to this period of his life. One was the American slant that the function of the railway was not in the first place to link one centre of population or industry with another, but for railways to *precede* settlement, to pioneer civilisation where there was none before. For Brassey, such would play a role in Australia from 1859. The other was the opportunity for the potential financing of the railway builder by the grant to him by, say, governments, of land alongside a line he was to build – real estate not in itself instantly contributive of cash-flow but a potential source of future income and a provider of collateral against which to borrow for the project in hand. His time to exploit that concept to the full was yet to come, notably in Argentina from 1864.

All this while, Brassey was facing the possibility of the Canadian government aborting its own baby, its Grand Trunk project, with the inevitable bankruptcy of the contractors. Once in Ottowa, the Federal capital, he set about negotiating various financial concessions with the Dominion government to keep the project rolling and at least notionally viable in the long term. (True viability would take another half-century.) With the scarcity of labour still pushing up the costs and slowing progress, he now turned back to his most dependable resource: he recruited and despatched across the Atlantic 3,000 British navvies, bricklayers, carpenters and masons whom he knew would do the job, at the highest level of productivity albeit at a cost which had not been in the original reckoning. The French Canadians recruited had proved to be nowhere near as strong as their British counterparts. By the later 1850s, senior engineer Hodges was substantially reinforcing human muscle power with steam-driven excavators bought in from the United States, somewhat to the scorn of the British labour contingent. But the excavators contributed decisively. Back in Britain, Brassey had pledged almost everything he possessed. He was appealing for a supreme effort to complete the bridge before 1859 was out.

The bridge was indeed opened for the first passage of trains on December 19 1859, and that mid-winter the Quebec-Toronto train service began to roll. *The Engineer* called Victoria Bridge 'the greatest example of engineering in the world'. The following summer HRH Prince Edward of Wales, visiting Canada for the purpose, declared of the Brassey consortium and its workforce: 'They left behind an imperishable monument of British skill, pluck, perseverance and science.' Indeed, but the consortium's partners had lost between them some £50 million (in today's values), and that nearly did for Peto and Betts.

All that half-decade, with various partners, Brassey had simultaneously been engaged in fulfilling contracts in Denmark, Italy, France, Austria, Spain, India, Australia, and throughout England. Barring Spain, all of these either had earned or would earn profits; and where Brassey was a shareholder, continuously so. There was no attempt to form a corporate Brassey entity: such would have served (we may assume) to complicate the book-keeping. Corporate tax had yet not reared its baleful head: a loss here would spare no tax on a profit there. One particular project, however, was fulfilled – with spectacular effect – at neither profit nor loss: in that unexpected peninsula which was to turn out to be the first major theatre of war for the British army since Waterloo in 1815, namely the Crimea. Let us cast a glance at that.

In 1854, Britain was approaching the zenith of its global power. Ossified and brittle, Ottoman Turkey's sultanic empire was looking frail enough to have inflated the ambitions of an expansionist Russia which had already occupied Ottoman Moldavia and Wallachia and had its eyes upon the Balkans. Britain, with Palmerston in the Cabinet, rallied to the defence of Turkey with a campaign to deny the Tsarist fleet their mastery of the Black Sea. This would entail the capture of the Russian naval base at Sevastopol on the Black Sea's north shore peninsula of Crimea. The British government, in alliance with the Turks and the French, had thus despatched some 30,000 men to Sevastopol's neighbouring bay of Balaclava.

The initial campaign of the summer months had proved chaotic and indecisive. Our troops were untried in war and poorly equipped. A quixotic supposition that experienced infantry, in the present case Russian, armed with muskets and powerful artillery, could be swept away by cavalry charges led by dashing fellows of the English upper classes brandishing sabres, had itself been swept away that late summer by the fiasco of the charge of the Light Brigade above Balaclava from which, out of 700 cavalrymen, a mere 195 returned[1] (among them the commander, Lord Cardigan, who galloped back through his lines to his yacht moored in Balaclava sound, took a bath and, not unreasonably, a bottle of champagne). '*C'est magnifique*,' was the sardonic observation of the French Marshal, Bosquet, '*mais ce n'est pas la guerre*.' The fast approaching winter threatened to be dour if not terrible. It was the latter.

The British people were getting to learn about all this through the despatches of a new medium of public enlightenment. This was provided by the foreign correspondent, and in the present instance the man from *The Times*, W H Russell. Conditions under which the troops were expected not merely to survive but also to fight, it was revealed to the folks at home, were appalling, and their logistical supply unforgivable in its incompetence and complacency. The materials once landed – be they warm clothing, food, medicine, shelter or weaponry – were taking weeks to reach the front line troops a few miles away, encircling Russian-held Sevastopol, since all roads had become a morass of mud. On November 14 had begun a fearful blizzard. The men in their thin clothing were hunched in tents without fuel. There was little food for either men or horses. The wounded commonly froze to death. Florence Nightingale, an unknown nursing superintendent of gentle birth who had talked her way into taking 38 women of her calling out to the Crimea and to her hospital base at Scutari, on the eastern shore of the Bosphorus, was about to sweep into the consciousness of the nation through the columns of *The Times*, which was doubtless present on the Brassey family's breakfast table.

Still buoyed by confidence in their far-flung operations, and with Birkenhead's Canada Works now in full swing, Brassey's consortium with Peto and Betts put it to the already rattled government of Lord Aberdeen that the Crimea supply problem could be overcome by building a railway from the quayside at Balaclava out along the entire length of the front, a track of 39 miles in all. The consortium declared that if given a free hand it would provide the railway *at cost*. A grateful administration – soon to be headed by Palmerston – accepted with relief. It was a gesture Brassey could soon scarcely afford; but he and his partners had made it, and they stuck to it.

---

[1] Recent research indicates that possibly half as many again survived, straggling back over the next few days.

In three days the trio of entrepreneurs had chartered two clippers, two paddle steamers, and four screw steamers including the 800-ton *Hesperus*. Canada Works could not provide instant rolling stock: whatever was additionally needed was bought. By mid-December, the advance party of 54 of Brassey's navvies had embarked on the clipper *Wildflower* each with his waterproof bag, a 'painted' suit, 3 cotton shirts, 2 flannel shirts, a flannel belt, a pair of moleskin trousers, a serge-lined moleskin vest, a Fearnaught slop (a kind of loose overgarment), a woollen coat, a pair of drawers, 2 cravats, a pair of leggings, stockings, regular boots, waterproof longboots, fishermen's boots, and hobnailed boots; a bed, pillow, 3 blankets and a rug; 2 pounds of tobacco and a portable stove. Each group got a waterproof hut.

The entire equipment for the proposed railway was under sail by the end of December, with a further contingent of 450 navvies – a complement later raised to 900. The flotilla had reached Balaclava by early February and the huts assembled in the snow in rows named Peto Terrace, Brassey Terrace, Preston Hall (after the enormous family house in Kent that Betts was building), Napoleon (to flatter the French), Victoria, Blackwell, Suffolk and Lancashire. Major-General Sir Henry Clifford wrote in a letter home that the navvies had the appearance of 'unutterable things' yet 'did more work in a day than a regiment of soldiers did in a week'. Characteristically, for Brassey, the logistical design was such that the track reached the very edge of the waterfront for cargo to be wheeled directly from the ships onto awaiting rolling stock.

In just over six weeks of Russian winter the railway was built. By the end of March 1855, 100 tons of shot and shell and 3,000 tons of clothing, blankets and medical supplies had reached the pitiably indigent soldiery. The partners had pulled their young chief engineer off a rail project in Nova Scotia: James Beatty had had virtually no sleep surveying the routes during the three weeks before the convoy arrived and while mastering the achievement throughout. On April 15 the train he was travelling in ran away on the steepish gradient from Balaclava Col, smashing into a stationary engine, killing one man and injuring Beatty seemingly ungravely. That December he was at last back in England and by March dead of an aneurism. He was 35. Meanwhile in September, Sevastopol had fallen to the British. Thomas Brassey was approaching 50. He never courted fame. But the nation had got to know his name and wondered at him.

⬭ ⬭ ⬭

India had come into Brassey's purview two years previously, in 1853, when
the Great Indian Peninsular and East Indian railways were begun under the
East India Company's administration and spurred by the vision of Lord
Dalhousie, Governor-General from 1848-56, a man after Brassey's heart,
who had perceived (from 1850) what railways could do to unify the
subcontinent in his charge. Brassey had sent out his trusted Stephen Ballard
to assess the potential; but when Ballard reported that government
engineers would supervise he went cold on the scheme. Brassey had learned
the lesson in Denmark of the practical ignorance and petty obstructiveness
of government *apparatchiks*. Fly-by-night contractors meanwhile tried their
luck, began work with neither capital enough nor organisation, built badly
and went bust. The Mutiny (1857) changed the Indian scene – and the
government structure. In 1858 came the opportunity for a key contract to
leapfrog a navigationally awkward 112-mile stretch of the Ganges above
Calcutta. Brassey went for it.

He took on Isambard Brunel as his consulting engineer in England, and
sent out Charles Henfrey to control the project on the ground. It lost him
money, that venture, because of the new imperial government's tardiness in
providing the land, and an unforeseen shortage of local labour forcing up the
wages. Yet the job was immaculately completed by 1862; and once in India,
Brassey saw fresh avenues, in particular to provide the arteries linking the
imperial capital at Delhi with Amritsar in Jammu and Kashmir to the north,
and south-eastwards with Calcutta. Both lines were to play their part in
shaping Indian history in the coming century. The northern line was to
become an engineering triumph, with the spanning of the wild Sutlej and the
Jumna rivers by stupendous viaducts – the Jumna's capricious switch of
course requiring an eleventh-hour doubling (to two kilometres) of its viaduct;
yet the line was completed well ahead of schedule and turned a threatening
loss into solid profit.

These Promethean endeavours, let us recall, were the achievement of an
'other-worldly' man: without hubris, quiet spoken, no swank in him, no
vanity, eschewing honours and the common appurtenances of success. It was
his partners and fellows who were busy building great houses – Peto's
Somerleyton, Betts' Preston Hall. Brassey held to his capital to invest in the
next project, the next venture or adventure, or to make good whenever for

any reason he needed to, should subcontractors fail or anything for which he felt responsible did not withstand the unpredicted test, as at Barentin. He resisted many an inducement to go in for what he would regard as speculative investments, albeit helping to finance his friend Isambard Brunel's scheme to build a ship, the *Great Eastern*, which would be six times the size of any vessel afloat at the time, in 1854[1]. As I have stressed, Brassey would never allow himself to fail to deliver what he had promised. To the ancient yeoman a reputation for probity and dependability was worth any gold.

When the Grand Trunk Railway virtually halved the fortune he then had, his only comment was that the family would have to tighten its belts until things took a turn for the better. He soon saw to it that things did. His had seen his earlier rivals and partners grow heady, spend on themselves, and pay the price. George Hudson, the precocious railway magnate of the early British boom – 'great swollen gambler' as Carlyle cast him – had overtraded and gone down a decade earlier. By early 1860, Peto and Betts were personally insolvent; with the bursting of the cotton bubble of 1866 and the collapse of the Overend and Gurney Bank that year, largely through the new generation of Gurneys' mismanagement, both of those particular erstwhile partners came financially to grief. Brassey survived the crash, if not without severe challenge – survived it, above all, by ignoring the urging of his long-faced comforters to cut his losses, quit the field and rest on past laurels.

Instead, he drove ahead with every one of the contracts he already had in hand. The biggest of these was jeopardised that very same year by Prussia's assault on his client, Austria, as I have told of in another context. But it was completing that further 165-mile line from Czernowitz (Chernovtsi) to Lemberg (Lviv) four months ahead of schedule, despite the odds stacked against the redemption of the bonds issued to finance the project, that secured him the release of £1 million (say, £50m today) at a critical juncture. That, and his ability to raise loans in the teeth of recession on the strength of his reputation, pulled him through. His existing railways were still earning. Even Thomas Brassey could feel the weight of work. Various of his fellow titans – Locke, Brunel, Robert Stephenson – had died in their fifties, relentlessly overworked. Yet new ventures were to roll on in Britain, where the railway surge had dwindled to a

---

[1] Eight years later, after its various misfortunes and Brunel's death, he was to buy the great ship, with Gooch and Barber, to serve as the layer of the first trans-Atlantic cable.

trickle, in Italy, Russia, Poland, Austria, Moldavia (newly a part of Rumania), Australia, Persia and, on a formidable scale, in Argentina[1]. By 1866 he had turned 60. And perhaps he was allowing himself a certain dream.

I have to hand six images of him: the earliest seated oil I have written of already, a drawing of the head (on the front cover of this essay) from his mid-forties, a lithograph (the title page), a three-quarter length daguerreotype (the back cover) from his early fifties, a later oil and a photograph. I see at once in the daguerreotype the cardinal attributes of human comportment in the scheme of things, namely calm, love, thanksgiving, and humour. He was manifestly loved and loving. I see fine eyes set wide, and in the eyes and mouth of every picture a kindness, integrity, and an easy generosity. Here is also authority without arrogance, sagacity without a trace of the paternal in the modern pejorative sense, and a genial surprise at what destiny had brought him without trace of hubris. There is a natural curl to the hair already thinning early. The commanding forehead of the younger man at length gives way to a bald top in the last picture. He is one we at once trust and are at ease with. 'Easy going'? 'Other-worldly'? That is what was said of him, was it not, by those of his hearth and blood, his intimates, just after he was gone.

He at last was allowing himself to dream a little through the surrogacy of his offspring. Tom had entered Parliament, for Devonport in 1865, and was soon to switch constituencies along the coast to Hastings in Sussex. In 1866 the young political aspirant bought a decent tract of land close to the battleground of that name where his ancestor from Brécey fought for and beside (so was the family's oral tradition) the future King William I of England. A wondrous house, even a château, was envisioned for the eldest son's progeny for ever, yet half-commemorative. Mediaeval revival, after all, was in the air. All three boys had a hand in it, and the dynastic founder Thomas now resided six or seven miles across the fields, at in St Leonards-on-Sea.

∞ ∞ ∞

It is May 1867. We find Thomas Brassey in Paris attending the Exhibition with a numerous group including several members of his family. He is 62,

---

[1] in whose railways' shares his grand-daughter, my grandmother Beatrice, had all of her inherited Brassey capital still invested when, in 1944, the pro Fascist *cuudillo*-in-the-making, Colonel Juan Peron, then Minister for Labour, expropriated the lot without compensation.

energy seemingly undiminished, health as robust as usual. He knows Paris. Much of his time here is taken up with business, yet he is ever enthusiastic as a sightseer. Sculpture he admires, and ceramics. He has long taken delight in giving dinner parties in the hotels he stays in, and does so now. On the day the party is to leave, he feels unwell. He typically refuses to alter his schedule, and the whole party takes the night train to Cologne, arriving at 4 am, where he insists they spend the hours until 9 am driving round the city and viewing the cathedral (which had taken an un-Brasseylike one hundred years to build).

He was back in England on June 7, and – in evidently weaker health – worked through the summer until early October when he was to attend the opening of the Mont Cenis Railway with its deep tunnel linking Italy and France through the Alps of Haute Savoie. Arriving at St Michel, the party was met by a blizzard of snow and fierce north winds. True to a form we are still familiar with, the French government had insisted adamantly that only French locomotives should be used on the line. One such engine was indeed on hand, with its carriages, for the inaugural journey. It broke down. Justifiably vexed, Brassey stood around in the cold and wet while a replacement engine was telegraphed for. When it arrived, it too failed. He was persuaded, under protest, to go back to the hotel at Lanslebourg, deeply despondent at the prospect of not now being able to keep his word on the promised formal opening of the line. That night he succumbed to bronchitis. With some difficulty he was carried to Turin for treatment. Maria and the family were informed by telegraph. They prepared to leave England at once, but then they heard that the object of their concern, still fevered, had insisted on proceeding to Milan and was now already *en route* to Venice where he had business. There the fever had risen to a new height. No sooner had it begun to abate than he concluded from his bed a critical deal deriving from the new Lemburg (Lviv)-Czernowicz (Chernovtsi) line.

Maria brought him home in stages to the family's leased home by the sea at St Leonards where, nominally resting, he continued to transact business brought to him from London. In early 1868 he suffered a stroke which left one leg dragging. It slowed him, but not by much. All his friends urged him to ease up, wind his projects down, devolve his responsibilities. His family had need of nothing; his achievements were vast, he had done his share, run the race. Yet something drove him on: an unremitting concern personally to keep faith not only with any contract that he had already entered upon but with all those accustomed to look to him for their daily bread and the exercise of the gifts that he had found in them: the core workforce of navvies. They had no protection from poverty once they were stood down. These men he knew and loved as the flesh-and-blood of their joint attainment; and there were towns and villages in the Midlands and the north of England that looked to him, depended on him, where he was simply revered.

In April 1969 he again set out on one of his comprehensive tours, to visit every one of his projects throughout Eastern Europe and the Balkans, in a seven-week journey of over 5,000 miles by every sort of conveyance – from Vienna to Styria; the prospective Predil tunnel; Trieste; by the Sommerag Pass back to Vienna; and immediately on to Budapest; to Giurgevo; and down the Danube to Bucharest and through Wallachia (Moldavia, today) to Jassy (Iasi) where cannons fired a salute for him and crowds lined the streets; and thence, with the sporting Ofenheim (a *Chevalier* now, with a *d'* before his name) to Czernowitz by his own line to Lemberg; and thence back across the continent to Paris. And, mark, there was yet a further East European trip that October.

In the spring of 1870 – he was 64 – his doctor told him he had cancer, from which at that time there was no reprieve.

He still declined to stop working and continued visiting his contractual sites in Britain, supervising the welfare of his men, shaking their hands at each site he attended upon: to them a greeting, for him an unspoken farewell. His very last railway project was – by the symmetry of fate – within a few miles of Penkridge Viaduct, site of his very first venture, in Staffordshire: the Wolverhampton to Walsall Railway.

That late summer of 1870 he took to his bed at home in St Leonards-on-Sea, in constant and mostly ferocious pain for which there was virtually no medical alleviation. Right up to the end his engineers and agents visited him; yet not only they. The navvies came too, several of them walking for days, village to village, to collect their fellows, to come south to pay their respects. As the hand of death began to close upon him, a knot of his navvies, lodging in the grounds, waited for the chance of seeing their old conjurer carried through the hall and out into his carriage for an airing: a still-breathing man transmuting into the stuff of myth.

Thomas Brassey died on December 8, 1870, of – precisely – a brain haemorrhage, in St Leonards' Victoria Hotel, a month beyond his 65th birthday, and was buried without pomp in the little churchyard at Catsfield, a few miles inland near his son Tom's new house. He had been crucially involved in the making of thousands of miles of railways worldwide, in changing the communication system of the nations and their neighbours, building the earth's greatest bridges, most elegant modern viaducts and longest tunnels, and in changing for ever social and economic patterns in virtually every country where he had pioneered the railway – in India, for example, fathering that honoured Anglo-Indian community which provides what are still today the arteries of the subcontinent; in Italy decisively contributing to the collective actuality of *il Risorgimento* and its final attainment of national unity in the year of his death. His obituaries were virtual eulogies to the man and his achievements, lauding his quiet, unswerving probity and unfailing dependability. Here was an exemplar of the work ethic and daring and undaunted enterprise of high Victorian England, stamping the consciousness of the world with the English *marque* of quality; of the will to surmount every obstacle to the righteous intent; and of the Englishman's word as binding.

Clearly, he was a driven man of unquenchable conviction in the morality of his endeavours: a morality of sheer standards of workmanship and ingenuity in the cause of human advancement. Yet equally clearly had he led less by driving those around him than by inspiring them, and personally responding to what the task faced *them* with. His own quiet presumption of loyalty to himself and the task in hand won that loyalty, in turn, from others, lifting his fellows at times to superhuman effort. He often had to, or chose to, work with men of a sharply contrasting cut – the *arriviste* Peto, for example, as a partner; or the Carlist brigand as a subcontractor on the Bilbao railway. When he picked his own engineers and managers, he picked aright; and there was that in him which won their trust, in some measure perhaps the underrunning Christian conviction of a 'profoundly religious' man (as the family described him). He would travel hundreds of miles in the flood of his activities to be with a sick or dying friend. In the end, his son Tom allowed himself at admit one flaw in Father: a reluctance to administer reproof even when vividly presented with the shortcomings of an employee or associate who had let him or a project down. Did that derive from a gentle perception of the inherent fallibility of man and the unshowy obligation of care for his fellows with which he knelt to pray? He was no Puritan. He was cheerfully thankful any bounty God might choose to bestow, and ensured a place of honour and a full plate for any chosen prelate who spoke the Grace at the banquets he threw from time to time on the fulfilment of a project or the overcoming of some great structural challenge.

He had married Maria Harrison in singleness of devotion, a woman of equivalent social origins and equivalent values, the trace of a shared brogue on her tongue. What she brought to him as companion, confidante, translator, mate and mother of his children was, as I have noted, a sustaining secret strength. She created new homes for him to fit the demands of his destiny, moving house again and again. She ran the households with calm efficiency and few pretensions, and saw to the early schooling of their three sons, Tom, Henry and Albert. Illustrious company, influence in high places, and wealth's glitter never jeopardized the couple's sturdy principles as so often they did among various of the magnates of Victorian industrial enterprise, including Brassey's own partners. He held to the root precepts of that south Cheshire race of farmers he sprang from; those roots held him.

At 12 or 13 the boys went as boarders to Dr Arnold's Rugby: a muscular Christianity that bred a duty to the common weal and the imperial mission. Thomas Brassey admired the speeches of Disraeli and Stanley (later Lord Derby). Tom and Henry both entered Parliament as – naturally enough for young men of their provenance – Liberals, albeit Liberals who were to transmute into Liberal Unionists which, by the century's end had merged as Unionists with the Tories: Henry at Dover[1]; and Tom, after Devonport and Hastings, then at St Andrew's in Liverpool. Henry died at 50. As for Tom, I sense that all his long life he had papa looking over his shoulder, checking on his progress: young Tom a figure of earnest endeavour, chronicler (in five volumes) of *The British Navy* and of *Work and Wages*, first published in 1872 (and read by that revolutionary Londoner of the time, Karl Marx). He had risen to the Secretaryship of the Admiralty by 1884-5, whereafter he lost his seat. He was compensated with a Peerage and soon a sinecure as a Lord-in-Waiting, and thence to govern Australia's state of Victoria (1895-1901). In due course, after a spell as President of the London Chamber of Commerce, he was offered an earldom on the accession of George V in 1911. His only son, Tab, felled by a taxi in 1919, survived him by a mere year, without issue. That Brassey title died with Tab, but was revived as a Peerage in the person of Henry's son (my great-uncle Leonard, of Apethorpe) in 1938, himself a Conservative and Unionist parliamentarian and a Party panjandrum.

---

[1] where I fought the seat under the successor Conservative and Unionist banner some 90 years later.

Thomas Brassey had died leaving £5.2 million in Britain alone – one of the largest English fortunes of the century, a figure we may calculate at comfortably in excess of £250 million in values of today. Though he and his Maria were not drawn to great possessions, he had acquired from his kinsman the old Brassey black-and-white house of Bulkeley in Cheshire, which he re-clad in the Victorian mode. In the last year of his life he bought the estate and the shell of the once magnificent early 18th century mansion at Heythrop, on Oxfordshire's border with Gloucestershire, as a wedding present for his third boy, Albert. Maybe he thought Albert could do with a challenge, since the whole interior had been burnt out in a conflagration in 1831. Albert duly restored Heythrop's splendour in the mode of his time. For each son the patronage and status that wealth bought was the reality of their existence. That's to say, they were perforce grandees. The three young men were swiftly established in their country houses. The politically aspiring Tom had already, by 1867, when Member for Hastings, built his superbly landscaped dream house Normanhurst, in French Second Empire style, with its lake and grottoes, sufficient to impress and entertain the great and the good, including of course his father in his last three years of life, and a generation or so later, as is still spoken of by the elderly of Battle, the last king of Hawaii.

Each had a London house – Albert, at 29 Berkeley Square, with its splendid ceilings; my great-grandfather Henry Brassey at Bath House, Piccadilly, with his country residence at what had been Betts' huge extravaganza, Preston Hall, near Aylesford in Kent, which Henry naturally improved. The snooty Pevsner, blind to the romance of the neo-Gothic, predictably described Preston Hall's ornamentation and mediaeval fancy as 'repellent in the extreme'. There my grandmother Beattie (Beatrice) grew up with her originally eleven siblings (three dying in infancy), to recall how on summer holiday visits to her Brassey cousins at Heythrop, the Henry Brasseys and their servants and their dogs would embark on their own train of three coaches in the grounds of Preston and chug their way on public rails (various of them built by grandfather Thomas), by-passing London proper by Brassey's Twickenham-Richmond line, to arrive at the halt at Charlbury or Chipping Norton station in the close proximity of Heythrop Park. There they played cricket, badminton and croquet out of doors and bezique, billiards or racquets when it rained, and rode ponies or hunted with their numerous cousins. My father David recalled holidaying there as a boy before the Great War, assembling before breakfast with the 105 members of household and estate staff for morning prayers conducted by great uncle Albert Brassey JP himself, who would then sound his hunting horn for the commencement of the day's activities. Memory of Albert lingers today – he died in 1918 – and his feudal style. Heythrop is now a swish country club. Preston Hall is a National Health Service administrative headquarters; and Normanhurst, this jewel of a home, this dream so devotedly and proudly made reality, after serving as a prisoner-of-war camp during the Second World War, and to spare Tom Brassey's daughter's heirs being fiscally raped by the Exchequer's Death Duty collectors was demolished in its entirety in 1951. *Sic transit gloria mundi*. Would Marx have smiled?

Newly rich grandees or no, Thomas's and Maria's sons and their offspring – those not priorly eliminated by childhood death or by the Germans in the Great War – married smoothly enough into the landed gentry or aristocracy without detectable social scrambling, joining the appropriate regiments and hunts and clubs, attending the appropriate schools, and here and there entering public life and taking up public office. An harmonious network was spreading scarcely perceptibly even to us further progeny. When I was at Eton in the 1940s, a dozen cousins of the Brassey gene overlapped my span there. Of that agnatic fold, few of us, I guess, knew much of the sweet genius that made us kin.

Of course, monuments to him abound all over the world in what he caused to be built, but they did not carry his name. (Was there not, in the righteous heart of this man, a sense of the Manichean presumption in the contrivances of engineering, however monumental? I suspect so.) Nor did the commercial structures he inaugurated carry his name. He is not commemorated on English high streets like his contemporary W H Smith, or in the names of shipping dynasties like Cayzer or Inchcape or fabricators like the Guests. There is a marble bust of him in a dedicated niche in the St Erasmus chapel in Chester's red-stone cathedral: that's all. Yet how dare the syllabus-devisers of our education system overlook him! What are the wells of their ignorance?

I do not absolve myself. Until I began to search him out with the bi-centenary looming, how little had I grown up to know of him. Some of us in the family speak of a genetic characteristic of the upper jaw as a 'Brassey mouth'; we come across a publishers of the Brassey name, initiated as a marine imprint by his son Tom who spent a fair proportion of his middle life in a rolling house party aboard his steam yacht *Sunbeam*, made famous through a popular chronicle *A Voyage in the Sunbeam*, 1878, by 'Lady Brassey', that is, his first wife Anna who died at sea off Darwin nine years later. Their vivid daughter Mary Adelaide was teased in a golfing quip for being not so much a 'brassie' as a 'driver' by her husband, the Viceroy of India, Lord Willingdon, whose viceregal premises in New Delhi she redecorated in mauve throughout, prompting its architect, Edwin Lutyens, to exclaim in dismay, *'Mauve qui peut!'* Do I digress? Certainly.

Glancing back a century or so I sense that all three sons, and several of the following generation of our forbears, whatever thrilling new blood had swum into the family's veins, spent their lives in the reflection of a rare and truly monumental original, Thomas Brassey, 1805-70, the greatest railway builder in the world. The next generation all but forgot him. This essay, marking the bi-centenary of his birth, calls on his many descendants today to clamour for his recognition. The mood is swinging back, is it not, to acknowledgement of the merit and motive of Britain's Victorian attainment. To sing our own ancestral unsung, do we not have a tribal duty, and perhaps patriotic one too, to make our voices heard?

T S July 2005

My sources include:

Sir Arthur Helps *Life and Labours of Mr Brassey*. First published 1872.
    Republished by Evelyn, Adams & Mackay, 1969
Charles Walker *Thomas Brassey: Railway Builder* Frederick Muller 1969
O S Nock *The Railway Engineers* Batsford 1955
John Millar *William Heap and his Company* John Millar (UK) Ltd, Hoylake 1976
L T C Rolt *Isambard Kingdom Brunel* Longmans Green 1957
J Mordaunt Crook *The Rise of the Nouveaux Riches* John Murray 1999
Michael Freeman *Railways and the Victorian Imagination* Hale University Press 1999
John Devey *Life of Joseph Locke* 1862
W G Sebald *The Rings of Saturn* Harvill 1998
Brian Cooke *The Grand Crimean Central Railway* Cavalier House, Knutsford 1997
Michael Chrimes et al. *Mackenzie – Giant of the Railways* Institution of Civil
    Engineers 1994
The family

Tom Stacey (www.tomstacey.com) is the author of seven novels, one filmed to his own screenplay; of collections of short stories; of three works of remote travel and ethnology including the most recently published *Tribe: the Hidden History of the Mountains of the Moon*; and of three books on current affairs. He is a former columnist, chief foreign correspondent of the *Sunday Times*, and winner of the Foreign Correspondent of the Year award. He won the John Llewellyn Rhys award for literature, and is a Fellow of the Royal Society of Literature. He was chief executive of the publishing house Stacey International from its inception in 1974 until 1999, since when he has remained non-executive chairman. In the field of penal reform, he is founder and Director of the Offender's Tag Association.

He is married to the sculptor Caroline Stacey, mother of their four daughters and one son, Sam, a civil engineer. They live in the house in Kensington from which I K Brunel chose his bride, Mary Horsley.